# THE EMPOWERED
# HIGHLY SENSITIVE PERSON'S JOURNAL

the
# EMPOWERED
# HIGHLY
# SENSITIVE
# PERSON'S
# JOURNAL

## 52 WEEKS
of Guided Prompts
for Self-Care

**APRIL SNOW,** LMFT

**ROCKRIDGE
PRESS**

For general information on our other products and services or to obtain technical support, please contact our Customer Care Department within the United States at (866) 744-2665, or outside the United States at (510) 253-0500.

Rockridge Press publishes its books in a variety of electronic and print formats. Some content that appears in print may not be available in electronic books, and vice versa.

TRADEMARKS: Rockridge Press and the Rockridge Press logo are trademarks or registered trademarks of Callisto Media Inc. and/or its affiliates, in the United States and other countries, and may not be used without written permission. All other trademarks are the property of their respective owners. Rockridge Press is not associated with any product or vendor mentioned in this book.

Art Producer: Samantha Ulban
Editor: Sean Newcott
Production Editor: Matthew Burnett
Production Manager: Jose Olivera

All images used under license © kloroform/Creative Market.
Author photograph courtesy of Lauren Selfridge and Tristan Brand.

Paperback ISBN: 978-1-63807-020-7
R0

THIS JOURNAL BELONGS TO

_____

# INTRODUCTION

**Despite so many things demanding your attention,** such as work, family, and social media, you've still managed to find this journal and take the first step in supporting yourself with more self-care. I imagine you might be starting from one of two places:

1. Prioritizing self-care is difficult, and you feel guilty when you set aside time for yourself.

2. You have plenty of time for self-care and are doing all the things (exercise, meditation, bodywork, etc.) you can, but still feel overwhelmed or unfulfilled.

Whether you're struggling to find time for self-care, feel overwhelmed most of the time, or are seeking more fulfillment in your life, this journal will help you discover the missing piece to your self-care puzzle. Most likely you're a highly sensitive person (HSP) needing the right kind or amount of self-care to support your unique temperament.

When you're born with the trait of high sensitivity, along with 20 percent of the population, you have different needs for rest and reflection (Lionetti et al., 2018). Why is that? HSPs have slight brain and nervous system differences that create more complex thinking and deep feelings, heightened perception, awareness of subtleties, and increased capacity for empathy (Acevedo et al., 2014).

Essentially, this means that you are more attuned to and affected by everything (and everyone) around you. Being so perceptive, empathetic, and aware can be a great asset at work and in your relationships, as well as allow you to have beautiful and complex life experiences. But without proper self-care and downtime, being highly sensitive will lead you straight to exhaustion, anxiety, stress, illness, a feeling of being overwhelmed, and a variety of other struggles.

As a highly sensitive introvert myself and a psychotherapist who specializes in working with highly sensitive people, I have witnessed time and time again the positive impact that intentional self-care and journaling can have for HSPs. My own personal practice includes yoga, meditation, and journaling each morning. This routine helps me feel grounded and connected to myself and is a helpful way to process thoughts and emotions.

Creating time for meaningful self-reflection and nurturing all the different parts of your experience (physical, emotional, mental, social, and spiritual) can help soothe the feeling of being overwhelmed that you may have become accustomed to, calm those big emotions, find clarity when your thoughts are jumbled, and nourish you on a deep emotional or spiritual level.

This journal was created with your unique highly sensitive needs in mind by taking an in-depth, holistic approach to the usual self-care practices. Each week, you'll have the opportunity to take a deep dive into one area of your life through positive affirmations, journal prompts, and experiential exercises. Through these guided practices, you'll discover new insights about yourself, reclaim the gifts of your sensitivity, and learn the right tools to manage your tendency to feel overwhelmed.

It's time to begin your self-care journey. Take your time as you move through this journal, focusing on one week at a time for a total of 52 weeks (or one full year). One of the best parts of being highly sensitive is being able to benefit more and grow from positive experiences (Belsky and Pluess, 2009). When you devote time to your self-care practice, you will feel the rewards in a big way. Grab a pen, and let's get started!

# Self-Care Basics for the Highly Sensitive Person

How often do you truly feel energized and fulfilled? If you're a highly sensitive person (HSP), you're more likely to feel overwhelmed, stressed, and exhausted most of the time. Most HSPs don't get the self-care and quiet downtime they need to survive, let alone thrive. Instead, they believe the messages from society, the media, or their own social circles that it's selfish or shows a lack of ambition to take time for themselves, and they feel guilty whenever they do. Trying to live up to the expectations of those who are not highly sensitive will only leave you feeling depleted— or worse—because stress can have a large impact on your physical, emotional, and mental health.

Because highly sensitive folks notice everything, feel deeply, and process their thoughts and experiences at length, you use a lot of emotional and physical energy that needs to be replenished *every day*. This means that the typical self-care routine of a massage here or a night out there doesn't even come close to meeting your needs. Instead, self-care is more about getting quiet on a daily basis and deeply nurturing your emotional, spiritual, intellectual, and physical needs.

Instead of the usual self-care practices, HSPs need to go a few steps deeper in not only frequency but also content. Examples of appropriate self-care practices for HSPs include:

→ Getting into nature
→ Connecting with animals
→ Self-reflection through journaling or psychotherapy
→ Emotionally rich connections with others
→ Reading engaging and inspirational books
→ Engaging in a spiritual or religious practice
→ Creating art, music, or poetry

The actual self-care practice isn't as important as how you feel when you're engaged with it. In addition to daily quiet time to reflect, what activities help you feel recharged, nourished, and inspired? Make sure you're practicing these weekly to clear away the noise of your busy life and recharge your inner battery.

When you practice self-care on a regular basis as an HSP, you'll notice that the feeling of being overwhelmed or stressed you've become accustomed to living with starts to fade away. In its place, you'll be able to access your sensitive gifts (creativity, empathy, intuition, etc.) and have more energy to engage in all areas of your life, work, and relationships.

## *Feeling deeply is a gift that allows me to experience great joy and connection.*

**SELF-CARE GOAL:** Begin to accept and welcome the range of my emotional experience, recognizing the gifts of feeling everything deeply, even when others may not understand my emotions.

What messages have I received about feeling deeply or having "big" emotions?

_____

_____

_____

_____

_____

_____

_____

_____

What would I like others to know about the complexity of my emotions?

_____

_____

_____

_____

_____

_____

_____

_____

_____

_____

_____

_____

_____

_____

_____

How does being more emotionally expressive benefit me?

_____

_____

_____

_____

_____

_____

_____

_____

Many HSPs have learned to push away, or repress, their "big" feelings because others don't understand them or are uncomfortable with them, but feeling deeply has the hidden advantage of giving you the ability to make well-informed decisions, experience immense joy, and connect deeply with others. For the next week, notice every time you have the urge to minimize or criticize your emotions. Then, instead of pushing away your feelings, practice this week's affirmation to remind yourself that whatever you're feeling makes sense and is valid.

*Learning about the trait I was born with helps me understand and take better care of myself.*

**SELF-CARE GOAL:** Educate myself on what it means to be a highly sensitive person and why I have different needs for rest and reflection. This will make it easier to practice self-care.

What have I learned about being highly sensitive?

_____

_____

_____

_____

_____

_____

_____

_____

_____

_____

In light of this new self-awareness, are there any self-care practices that could feel supportive to my HSP self?

_____

_____

_____

_____

_____

_____

_____

_____

_____

_____

_____

_____

_____

_____

With this new way of perceiving myself, in what ways do I now understand my past experiences and relationships differently?

_____

_____

_____

_____

_____

_____

_____

_____

_____

_____

_____

Look over the resources list on page 158 and begin reading a book of your choosing on the highly sensitive person, or watch the documentary *Sensitive: The Untold Story.* Afterward, reflect on what you have learned about yourself using the journaling prompts for this week.

# I am relaxed and ready for sleep.

**SELF-CARE GOAL:** Create a soothing, quiet, and cozy space where I can fall asleep effortlessly and without distractions.

When I look around my sleep space, what keeps me awake is . . .

_____

_____

_____

_____

_____

_____

_____

_____

_____

_____

_____

What changes do I need to make in my sleep space to fall asleep more easily?

_____

_____

_____

_____

_____

_____

_____

_____

_____

_____

_____

_____

_____

_____

How has adjusting my sleep space changed my quality of sleep and relationship to bedtime?

_____

_____

_____

_____

_____

_____

_____

_____

As you try to fall asleep over the next week, make note of anything that's keeping you from feeling relaxed. You may find it helpful to use curtains to reduce excess light; change your bedding to something more comfortable; tack up blankets, add an area rug, or install soundproofing panels to reduce noise; or use a fan, white noise machine, or anything else that would help you feel more supported. After you have implemented these changes, reflect on any differences you notice in your quality of sleep, mood, or energy levels.

*There are other highly sensitive people who experience the world as I do; I'm not alone.*

**SELF-CARE GOAL:** Begin to build relationships with other highly sensitive people to feel more fully understood and accepting of myself.

Spending time with other highly sensitive people feels . . .

_____

_____

_____

_____

_____

_____

_____

_____

_____

_____

The difference between connecting with HSPs and folks who aren't highly sensitive is . . .

_____

_____

_____

_____

_____

_____

_____

_____

_____

_____

_____

_____

_____

_____

_____

What is important to me about connecting with other HSPs?

_____

_____

_____

_____

_____

_____

_____

_____

_____

_____

_____

Create opportunities for connection with other highly sensitive people. You can approach this by searching for local HSP support or social groups on meetup.com, starting a local or virtual book club, hosting a viewing of the documentary _Sensitive: The Untold Story_ at your local library, or joining online HSP communities.

*I live a purposeful life filled with intention and clarity; my path is clear.*

**SELF-CARE GOAL:** Discover or reconnect with what feeds my soul.

During the time of my life when I felt most fulfilled, what was happening?

_____

_____

_____

_____

_____

_____

_____

_____

_____

_____

What am I doing, who am I with, and where am I when I feel most alive?

_____

_____

_____

_____

_____

_____

_____

_____

_____

_____

_____

_____

_____

_____

_____

To feel more purpose in my current life, I need . . .

_____

_____

_____

_____

_____

_____

_____

_____

_____

_____

Going back through your life's memories, photos, videos, or journals, take note of the times you felt most purposeful and excited about what you were doing. Using the journaling prompts from this week, begin to identify what adjustments you may want to make to bring yourself toward greater purpose.

# My feelings are valid and worthy of expression.

**SELF-CARE GOAL:** Begin to soften messages from my inner critic, which says my emotions are unwelcome, and instead embrace how I'm feeling in each moment.

What is my inner critic saying?

_____

_____

_____

_____

_____

_____

_____

_____

_____

_____

_____

If my inner critic were protecting me from something, what would it be?

_____

_____

_____

_____

_____

_____

_____

_____

_____

_____

_____

_____

_____

What do I need my inner critic to know about how I'm feeling right now?

_____

_____

_____

_____

_____

_____

_____

_____

_____

Your inner critic is often a cautious caregiver in disguise, wanting you to play it safe to avoid conflict or disappointment. Practice this week's affirmation whenever you notice that little voice inside pushing you to hide your emotions, and let your inner critic know what you need instead. As you slowly begin to release the urge to criticize or reject your emotional experiences, notice if you are able to be present and validate those emotions instead by saying, "This makes sense. Of course I feel this way."

## *I am enough, and I am doing enough.*

**SELF-CARE GOAL:** Reframe the message I've heard that relaxing and taking my time means I'm "unmotivated" or "not enough."

Where did these narratives that rigidly connect productivity and worth come from?

_____

_____

_____

_____

_____

_____

_____

_____

_____

_____

How would I advise a friend who was receiving these critical messages?

_____

_____

_____

_____

_____

_____

_____

_____

_____

_____

_____

_____

_____

_____

_____

_____

Why is it important for me to rest on a regular basis?

_____

_____

_____

_____

_____

_____

_____

_____

_____

_____

Over the next week, notice any social pressures or internal narratives that come up around the idea of doing "enough." Repeat the affirmation to yourself and see if there is space to treat yourself as you would a friend in the same position. Using the journal prompts for this week, get curious about the origin of these internal messages and remind yourself of the importance of resting.

*My mind is quiet and still; I feel completely present in this moment.*

**SELF-CARE GOAL:** Enjoy time to decompress without the pressure of staying busy. Give my body time to relax and my mind time to settle.

How do I feel about slowing down and doing nothing?

_____

_____

_____

_____

_____

_____

_____

_____

_____

What do I enjoy most during quiet moments to myself?

_____

_____

_____

_____

_____

_____

_____

_____

_____

_____

_____

_____

When I set aside time to mindfully relax, what changes do I notice in my mood, focus, or energy levels?

_____

_____

_____

_____

_____

_____

_____

_____

For the next week, set aside at least 20 minutes each day to sit quietly without distractions. You could spend the time practicing mindfulness by following your breath as it moves in and out. You may also find joy in birdwatching in a local park, in a parking lot during a work break, or on your front steps. Other ideas include slowly sipping a cup of tea at sunrise or sunset and resting quietly in a place with a peaceful environment where you best feel you can access nature. No matter how you decide to spend the time, give yourself permission to slow down and notice the effects of this exercise using this week's journaling prompts.

*I feel safe to share my sensitivity with others and am ready to be understood by those around me.*

**SELF-CARE GOAL:** Be seen as a highly sensitive person and feel more fully understood as my whole self.

Who are the people in my life that I would consider sharing my sensitivity with?

_____

_____

_____

_____

_____

_____

_____

_____

_____

What do I want to say about my experiences of being a highly sensitive person?

_____

_____

_____

_____

_____

_____

_____

_____

_____

_____

_____

_____

_____

_____

When I openly talk about being an HSP, what shifts in me or in my relationships with others?

_____

_____

_____

_____

_____

_____

_____

_____

_____

If possible, choose one person you trust to share your experiences as a highly sensitive person. Together, you could watch _Sensitive: The Untold Story_ or take the HSP self-test (see the resources list on page 158). If that's not possible, tell them about one characteristic you have because you're highly sensitive. Reflect on the experience of opening up about your sensitivity using this week's journaling prompts.

*I trust my intuition in times
of uncertainty.*

**SELF-CARE GOAL:** Begin to tune in to the heightened intuition so common for HSPs like myself.

Reflecting back, when have my instincts been accurate?

_____

_____

_____

_____

_____

_____

_____

_____

_____

_____

What happens when I ignore my intuition?

_____

_____

_____

_____

_____

_____

_____

_____

_____

_____

_____

_____

_____

How about when I trust my inner wisdom?

_____

_____

_____

_____

_____

_____

_____

_____

_____

_____

Highly sensitive people are very perceptive and intuitive, but will often doubt themselves because others will miss the cues HSPs so easily pick up on. Begin to notice when you have hunches, gut instincts, or other sensations about a situation, person, or decision you have to make. Reflect on your relationship with trusting or not trusting your intuition in the past, in order to better help you understand this experience.

## *My hobbies are meaningful and I have time to enjoy them.*

**SELF-CARE GOAL:** Reconnect with a hobby with which I have a positive emotional connection, such as a sport or instrument I played in childhood or a skill that I learned from a grandparent or mentor.

This hobby reminds me of . . .

_____

_____

_____

_____

_____

_____

_____

_____

_____

_____

When I spend time doing this activity, I feel and notice . . .

_____

_____

_____

_____

_____

_____

_____

_____

_____

_____

_____

_____

_____

_____

Reconnecting with this hobby is important to me because . . .

_____

_____

_____

_____

_____

_____

_____

_____

_____

_____

Allow yourself to intentionally reminisce about your favorite hobbies from childhood (or adulthood) and then choose one of those activities and set aside time this week to engage in it. Reflect on how it feels to reconnect with this hobby and what you notice about your emotional experience using this week's journal prompts.

# I can find a place for everything in my schedule.

**SELF-CARE GOAL:** Reduce the decision fatigue I might have about "what to do when" by creating a regular weekly routine with space for all my recurring tasks, such as self-care, meal prep, laundry, and so forth.

My weekly schedule is as follows . . .

_____

_____

_____

_____

_____

_____

_____

_____

_____

_____

_____

What tasks am I doing more than once per week?

_____

_____

_____

_____

_____

_____

_____

How can I consolidate tasks so I am doing them less often?

_____

_____

_____

_____

_____

_____

_____

What changes do I notice in focus and mental clarity when I batch tasks together and maintain a weekly routine?

_____

_____

_____

_____

_____

_____

_____

_____

_____

_____

Because HSPs process decisions at length and need more transition time between tasks, you can spare yourself a lot of mental energy by creating a consistent weekly routine. It helps to have similar tasks such as laundry and cooking batched together. Write out your weekly schedule, consolidating repetitive tasks. Then spend time reflecting on the impact you feel after creating changes to your routine. Notice what feels supportive and what needs to be further adjusted.

# By taking care of my body, I take care of my mind and emotions.

**SELF-CARE GOAL:** Use physical movement to help process my thoughts and emotions.

Back-and-forth motions such as walking, running, dancing, drumming, water aerobics, adapted yoga, or simply tapping from left to right on any surface can be especially helpful. What types of physical movement have I tried in the past that helped clear my mind or boost my mood?

_____

_____

_____

_____

_____

_____

_____

_____

_____

On a typical day, when could I find time to increase my physical activity?

_____

_____

_____

_____

_____

_____

_____

_____

_____

_____

_____

_____

_____

_____

When I incorporate movement into my self-care practice, the impact I notice is . . .

_____

_____

_____

_____

_____

_____

_____

Whenever you're feeling scattered, stressed, or upset over the next week, try adding gentle back-and-forth movement to help you process. This could look like going on a midday walk to de-stress from work, tapping back and forth on the kitchen counter while you wait for dinner to cook and think about your day, or inviting your loved ones to take a five-minute dance break to bring levity after an argument. Whether practicing alone or with a friend, imagine releasing the stress from your body as you move and use the affirmation to remind yourself why it's important to include physical movement to support your emotional and mental health.

## Connecting deeply brings meaning and fulfillment to my relationships.

**SELF-CARE GOAL:** Experience fewer draining or awkward exchanges, and more meaningful connections in new or existing relationships.

The thought of having a shallow conversation with someone makes me feel . . .

_____

_____

_____

_____

_____

_____

_____

_____

_____

_____

When I give myself permission to skip the small talk, I notice . . .

_____

_____

_____

_____

_____

_____

_____

_____

_____

_____

_____

_____

_____

How do others respond when I ask more complex, engaging questions?

_____

_____

_____

_____

_____

_____

_____

_____

_____

During your next conversation, ask a more specific question about topics you're interested in instead of the usual small talk. This could include inquiring about someone's pet, favorite author, travels, or movie preferences. Use open-ended questions that require more than a "Yes" or "No" answer, starting off with phrases such as "Tell me about..." or "What is your opinion on...?" Notice what feels different about the exchange compared to more superficial connections.

*I feel calmed and soothed by the stillness and serenity of nature around me.*

**SELF-CARE GOAL:** Mindfully connect with a place in nature that is meaningful to me in order to step away from the busyness of life and experience a sense of deep quiet and introspection.

The places in nature where I feel the most serene and connected to myself are . . .

_____

_____

_____

_____

_____

_____

_____

_____

_____

As I look around this outdoor space, I notice . . .

_____

_____

_____

_____

_____

_____

_____

_____

_____

_____

_____

_____

_____

_____

_____

_____

_____

When I allow myself time to fully be present in the natural world, how do I feel afterward?

_____

_____

_____

_____

_____

_____

_____

_____

This week, schedule a time to spend at least 30 to 60 minutes outdoors—or in another place where you feel comfortable and in tune with nature—without interruption. You could choose to be in the woods, visit the ocean, or find a remote bench at the park. As if you were a child, look around and really notice the subtle details of the place you find yourself in. Allow yourself to be fully present with the sounds, sights, smells, and textures. Afterward, spend a few moments journaling about your experience.

# *My body tells me when it's time to take a break.*

**SELF-CARE GOAL:** Begin to identify the signs that signal I am emotionally overwhelmed (e.g., irritable, anxious, exhausted, etc.) and take time to rest.

I know I am overwhelmed when . . .

_____

_____

_____

_____

_____

_____

_____

_____

_____

_____

What I need most during times when I feel overwhelmed is . . .

_____

_____

_____

_____

_____

_____

_____

_____

_____

_____

_____

_____

_____

If I don't take care of myself, what will happen next is . . .

_____

_____

_____

_____

_____

_____

_____

_____

_____

_____

A tendency to feel overwhelmed is a common experience for HSPs but shows up differently for everyone. A few common signs are increased irritability, anxiety, exhaustion, restlessness, headaches, and indigestion. This week, track your unique signs of having too much to deal with and be sure to take breaks as needed. Breaks could include closing your eyes for a few moments, taking some time outside to get fresh air, or setting a boundary with a loved one to get some alone time.

# I enjoy taking the space to think and reflect.

**SELF-CARE GOAL:** Get at least 20 minutes of downtime every day to process my experiences and check in with my mental health.

What differences do I notice in my energy when I get downtime?

_____

_____

_____

_____

_____

_____

_____

_____

_____

What difference do I notice in my ability to focus when I get downtime?

_____

_____

_____

_____

_____

_____

_____

_____

_____

_____

_____

_____

_____

What difference do I notice in my mental state when I get downtime?

_____

_____

_____

_____

_____

_____

_____

_____

_____

Every day this week, set aside at least 20 minutes to relax and do nothing. You can gaze out the window, daydream, lounge in a comfortable spot outdoors, drink a cup of tea, or spend some time in nature. No matter what you choose to do, just let your mind wander without any agenda. You may feel resistance to slowing down at first, or hear a lot of mental chatter amid the quiet; that is to be expected. Give yourself time to get comfortable being still, leaning on this week's affirmation in the meantime.

*The space around me feels calming and soothing to my senses.*

**SELF-CARE GOAL:** Reduce causes of overstimulation in any environment where I spend a significant amount of time, such as at home, at work, or in the car.

What feels overstimulating (too bright, loud, rough, cluttered, etc.) when I look around my home, work space, or vehicle?

_____

_____

_____

_____

_____

_____

_____

What changes would make my environment more soothing and relaxing?

_____

_____

_____

_____

_____

_____

_____

_____

_____

_____

_____

_____

_____

How do I feel once these changes have been implemented?

_____

_____

_____

_____

_____

_____

_____

_____

_____

Over the next week, start to observe your surroundings when you feel irritable, frazzled, anxious, or overstimulated in any way. Identify possible sources of sensory overstimulation, such as bold colors or bright overhead lighting, itchy textures on pillows or furniture, or excessive clutter. Make any adjustments you can to reduce sources of overstimulation, remembering that the changes don't have to be perfect to have an impact.

# People will understand and appreciate me just as I am.

**SELF-CARE GOAL:** Begin to reframe the narrative that I am always misunderstood as a highly sensitive person and remind myself that connection with other HSPs is possible.

When have I felt understood in a current or past relationship of any kind?

_____

_____

_____

_____

_____

_____

_____

_____

_____

_____

That connection reminds me that . . .

_____

_____

_____

_____

_____

_____

_____

_____

_____

_____

_____

_____

_____

_____

What I need to feel supported in relationships with others is . . .

_____

_____

_____

_____

_____

_____

_____

_____

_____

_____

Because HSPs make up approximately 20 percent of the population, and because each person is unique, feeling misunderstood is common. But it's important to remind yourself that feeling understood is possible. Such possibilities exist with other HSPs and with people who aren't highly sensitive but who are supportive and understanding. Over the next week or so, look for small moments of feeling seen or sharing experiences in your current or past relationships.

## *Even as an adult, I am carefree and full of childlike wonder.*

**SELF-CARE GOAL:** Be fully present during a creative and tactile experience such as collage, finger paints, clay, shadow puppets, or sailing paper boats, just as a child would.

What is my relationship with creativity and play?

_____

_____

_____

_____

_____

_____

_____

_____

_____

_____

When I was a child, my favorite ways to express myself were . . .

_____

_____

_____

_____

_____

_____

_____

_____

_____

_____

_____

_____

_____

_____

_____

Tapping into my inner child's creativity helped me remember or realize . . .

_____

_____

_____

_____

_____

_____

_____

_____

_____

_____

Set aside a few hours to fully immerse yourself in a creative activity. Try to focus your energy on having fun and being curious, as a child might, setting aside any judgments or expectations. The goal is not to produce art, but to be present to the experience and reconnect with your carefree, childlike self. Reflect on your relationship with creativity, play, and expression using this week's journal prompts.

# I bestow upon myself the empathy I freely give to others.

**SELF-CARE GOAL:** Empathize with my own emotional experiences as I would those of a friend or loved one.

What would I say or do for a loved one experiencing my struggles?

_____

_____

_____

_____

_____

_____

_____

_____

_____

_____

_____

_____

When I offer myself empathy, I am aware of . . .

_____

_____

_____

_____

_____

_____

_____

_____

_____

_____

_____

_____

_____

_____

_____

_____

_____

_____

_____

_____

_____

_____

_____

_____

Imagine a dear friend or family member feeling what you're experiencing today or this week. Take all that empathy you would lovingly give to them and offer it to yourself. This could be in the form of kind, supportive words, or acts of service such as buying dinner after a rough day at work. Pause to notice how it feels to be the recipient of empathy rather than the giver.

# I pause to rest between tasks to allow my mind space to process.

**SELF-CARE GOAL:** Adopt the habit of creating a meaningful pause between tasks to allow space to reflect before transitioning to the next activity.

The most difficult part of hitting pause is . . .

_____

_____

_____

_____

_____

_____

_____

_____

_____

_____

When I allow myself space to pause and reflect between tasks, I notice . . .

_____

_____

_____

_____

_____

_____

_____

_____

_____

_____

_____

_____

_____

_____

The benefit of slowing down between activities is . . .

_____

_____

_____

_____

_____

_____

_____

_____

_____

Over the next week, practice pausing after each activity and taking a short break every one or two hours. You can take a few deep breaths, close your eyes for a moment, do a few stretches, or whatever else would feel energizing and soothing. The longer you have been focused, the longer the break. For instance, you may only need a few minutes after checking email for an hour, but may desire a longer break if you've been cleaning the house for two hours.

# The way I dress my body feels comforting.

**SELF-CARE GOAL:** Create an HSP-friendly wardrobe by choosing clothes on the basis of comfort.

How do I want to feel in my clothing?

_____

_____

_____

_____

_____

_____

_____

_____

_____

Do the items I have meet that need?

_____

_____

_____

_____

_____

_____

_____

_____

_____

_____

_____

_____

_____

_____

_____

_____

What types of fabrics, textures, or colors would feel most comfortable?

_____

_____

_____

_____

_____

_____

_____

_____

_____

_____

Spend time this week sorting through your closet, drawers, or wherever you store the clothing you wear most often. Start by cutting out annoying tags and donate anything that is irritating, scratchy, tight, or too bright. As you look at the clothing you have that does feel comfortable, notice what similarities there are in terms of type of fabric, style, colors, or patterns. Over time, as financial resources and space allow, incorporate more of these types of clothing items into your wardrobe.

*I only say yes to a social invitation when I have the bandwidth and availability.*

**SELF-CARE GOAL:** Limit my weekly number of social commitments so that I am only engaging with others when I have the energy and interest.

How many social activities can I commit to each week without feeling drained or resentful?

_____

_____

_____

_____

_____

_____

_____

_____

_____

_____

What is the impact on myself and my relationships when I *don't* honor my needs?

_____

_____

_____

_____

_____

_____

_____

_____

_____

_____

_____

_____

_____

What is the impact on myself and my relationships when I *do* honor my needs?

_____

_____

_____

_____

_____

_____

_____

_____

_____

_____

As you move through this week, notice how you feel during social engagements or when you receive social invitations. Do you feel pressure to say "yes" when you really need or want to say "no"? Were you okay with two get-togethers, but the third left you feeling exhausted? Using the journal prompts, begin to reflect on your own social needs and boundaries.

*I am in awe of the beauty in this piece of art.*

**SELF-CARE GOAL:** Allow myself the pleasure of being fully present with the beauty of art in any form (e.g., painting, ballet, theater, etc.).

How does art or any other type of creative expression tend to affect me?

_____

_____

_____

_____

_____

_____

_____

_____

_____

_____

When I'm immersed in the experience of actively engaging with art, I am aware of . . .

_____

_____

_____

_____

_____

_____

_____

_____

_____

_____

_____

_____

_____

_____

_____

_____

_____

_____

_____

_____

_____

_____

_____

Clear away any distractions to spend a few hours visiting an art museum, picking up an art or photography book from the library, or attending a live theater or dance performance in person or online. Slow down to notice your experience in the moment, particularly the thoughts, emotions, sensations, or images that are present for you. Spend time journaling about your experience.

## My feelings are just right, and I welcome all my emotions.

**SELF-CARE GOAL:** Slowly rewrite the narrative that my feelings are "too much." Begin to be present to my emotions and allow myself to express them through words, tears, movement, or art.

Where did I learn that my feelings (positive or negative) could be "too much"?

_____

_____

_____

_____

_____

_____

_____

_____

_____

_____

In what ways would I like to try expressing my emotions?

_____

_____

_____

_____

_____

_____

_____

_____

_____

_____

_____

_____

_____

Being present to my full emotional expression feels like . . .

_____

_____

_____

_____

_____

_____

_____

_____

_____

Next time you notice yourself minimizing or pushing away
your feelings, see if there's room to express yourself authen-
tically and openly through words, tears, movement, writing,
or art. This might include laughing out loud, crying, using your
voice to express to someone what you're feeling and why
that's important, dancing it out, journaling, writing a story, or
creating art. You get to decide what type of expression would
feel best and who to share your emotional experiences with.
Use this week's journal prompts to help you along the way.

# I feel best when I slowly ease into my day.

**SELF-CARE GOAL:** Set aside time to start the day slowly and with focus, instead of feeling frazzled and rushed.

What gets in the way of starting the day slowly and mindfully?

_____

_____

_____

_____

_____

_____

_____

_____

_____

_____

_____

How does easing into the day (versus rushing) affect my mood for the rest of the day?

_____

_____

_____

_____

_____

_____

_____

_____

_____

_____

_____

_____

_____

How does easing into the day affect my mental state for the rest of the day?

_____

_____

_____

_____

_____

_____

_____

_____

_____

Try carving out at least five minutes in the morning to linger in bed and reflect on the day ahead. You may need to go to bed slightly earlier the night before so you don't lose sleep. Using the journal prompts for this week, reflect on the barriers to taking this time for yourself, such as your mindset, external pressures, or other responsibilities. Then notice how creating space has an effect on how you feel through the rest of the day, and can elevate your mood, energy, and mental state.

*Today I can completely relax; there's nowhere I have to be and nothing I have to do.*

**SELF-CARE GOAL:** Spend an entire day in pajamas or comfortable clothes to signify that it's a relaxation day.

When I give myself permission to fully relax, I notice . . .

_____

_____

_____

_____

_____

_____

_____

_____

_____

The best part of today was . . .

_____

_____

_____

_____

_____

_____

_____

_____

_____

_____

_____

_____

_____

_____

_____

_____

_____

_____

_____

_____

_____

_____

_____

_____

_____

If you are able, find a 12- to 24-hour period to let everyone know you're unavailable, turn off your phone, and settle in for a day of cozy relaxation. You can have a movie marathon, read all day, dive into a puzzle, craft, catch up on sleep, or do whatever would feel restorative for you. End the day by journaling about how the experience felt for you.

# *I choose the best times I am available.*

**SELF-CARE GOAL:** Intentionally set the times I am available for contact and socializing so I have enough time for my self-care practices.

My concerns about setting boundaries are . . .

_____

_____

_____

_____

_____

_____

_____

_____

_____

_____

_____

What feels different when I limit my availability and prioritize myself?

_____

_____

_____

_____

_____

_____

_____

_____

_____

_____

_____

_____

_____

_____

_____

_____

_____

_____

_____

_____

_____

_____

_____

Considering your needs for quiet reflection and rest, choose
the times of day and the days of the week that you want to
be available to socially connect with others. Let your friends,
family, and coworkers know which hours and days you will be
off-limits. Setting boundaries can bring up feelings of guilt or
worry, which is a sign of how much you care about others, but
remember that setting limits is essential to keeping yourself
available to your relationships over the long term.

*I am inspired and enlivened by the intricacies of my favorite music.*

**SELF-CARE GOAL:** Use music to connect deeply with myself and feel how it affects me on a spiritual and emotional level.

How has music influenced or supported me throughout different moments in my life?

_____

_____

_____

_____

_____

_____

_____

_____

_____

_____

What feelings do the lyrics of my favorite song evoke in me?

_____

_____

_____

_____

_____

_____

_____

_____

_____

_____

_____

_____

_____

_____

_____

_____

_____

_____

_____

_____

_____

_____

_____

_____

_____

_____

_____

Connect with yourself this week by visiting a local record store, attending an intimate live performance (whether in person or online), or creating an inspirational playlist. Clear everything away, close your eyes, and really listen. Journal about what comes up for you during this practice of being immersed in your favorite music.

# I hear what my emotions are telling me and will honor my needs.

**SELF-CARE GOAL:** Listen to what my emotions are telling me as a way to begin to prioritize my self-care needs.

What is my current emotion communicating to me?

_____

_____

_____

_____

_____

_____

_____

_____

_____

_____

_____

This feeling shows up when . . .

_____

_____

_____

_____

_____

_____

_____

_____

_____

_____

_____

_____

_____

_____

_____

_____

_____

_____

_____

_____

_____

_____

_____

_____

_____

Notice when emotions such as joy, sadness, or anger arise. Observe the circumstances—what you're doing, where you are, and who else is there. Then reflect on what your feelings may be trying to tell you. Do you need to set a boundary? Are you overstimulated? Have you overcommitted yourself and your time?

# Reflecting on my day allows my mind to settle.

**SELF-CARE GOAL:** Have enough time before bedtime to reflect on the day's events and feel mentally relaxed enough to fall asleep easily.

Today's highlights are . . .

_____

_____

_____

_____

_____

_____

_____

_____

_____

_____

What went well today?

_____

_____

_____

_____

_____

_____

I was frustrated when . . .

_____

_____

_____

_____

_____

_____

_____

_____

Tomorrow I want to focus on . . .

_____

_____

_____

_____

_____

_____

_____

_____

_____

_____

_____

Intentionally get into bed at least 15 to 20 minutes before you want to fall asleep. Spend a few minutes journaling about your day using this week's journal prompts. Notice how processing your day affects your ability to fall asleep and how you feel the next morning.

# I feel soothed and relaxed by my own gentle touch.

**SELF-CARE GOAL:** Use gentle self-touch to soothe my frazzled nerves during times of stress, heightened emotions, or feeling overwhelmed.

The type of touch that I find the most soothing is . . .

_____

_____

_____

_____

_____

_____

_____

_____

_____

_____

_____

Receiving this self-touch feels . . .

_____

_____

_____

_____

_____

_____

_____

_____

_____

_____

_____

_____

_____

_____

_____

_____

_____

_____

_____

_____

_____

_____

_____

_____

_____

_____

During times of stress, offer yourself comfort through gentle self-touch. You may find it soothing to place a hand over your heart or on your cheeks, wrap your arms around your torso, massage the back of your neck or feet, or, if you are able to, bring your knees up to your chest.

# I say "no" and set limits on my social time without feeling guilty.

**SELF-CARE GOAL:** Practice setting boundaries this week by checking my energy levels and setting limits when I need rest or alone time.

When I honor my needs and actively set boundaries, I feel . . .

_____

_____

_____

_____

_____

_____

_____

_____

_____

_____

_____

_____

Saying no when I'm tired or need alone time is okay because . . .

_____

_____

_____

_____

_____

_____

_____

Setting boundaries allows me to . . .

_____

_____

_____

_____

_____

_____

_____

If a friend were struggling with prioritizing their needs, I would encourage them to . . .

_____

_____

_____

_____

_____

_____

_____

_____

_____

_____

This week, practice pausing before you say "yes" to a social invitation or request. Ask yourself, "Do I have the energy and time to engage, or do I need to decline this invitation?" If you are feeling guilty for saying "no," practice this week's affirmation and offer yourself the same compassion you would offer to a friend in the same situation.

# My dreams contain important insights into my feelings and needs.

**SELF-CARE GOAL:** Slow down each morning to reflect on my dreams and any messages they may contain.

Write down some details from one of last night's dreams . . .

_____

_____

_____

_____

_____

_____

_____

_____

_____

_____

The feeling that dream left me with is . . .

_____

_____

_____

_____

_____

_____

_____

_____

_____

_____

_____

_____

_____

If I had to guess, this dream is telling me . . .

_____

_____

_____

_____

_____

_____

_____

_____

_____

_____

Dreams are often vivid and emotionally rich for HSPs, an extension of the deep processing your mind does. When you wake up, spend a few minutes reflecting on the journal prompts from this week to discover if there's anything meaningful to take from your dreams before you move into the rest of your day.

# I recognize and understand my emotional reactions.

**SELF-CARE GOAL:** Become aware of what emotions are present in me and begin to understand when and why I tend to feel them.

What are the circumstances (time, place, person, etc.) when a particular emotion, such as fear or anger, is present?

_____

_____

_____

_____

_____

_____

_____

_____

_____

_____

_____

Why might this emotion be surfacing now?

_____

_____

_____

_____

_____

_____

_____

_____

_____

_____

_____

_____

_____

_____

Are there any actions I need to take to feel safer or get my needs met?

_____

_____

_____

_____

_____

_____

_____

_____

_____

_____

Pretend you are an investigator looking for clues. Begin to notice what causes or intensifies your emotions to better understand your own rhythms, and take time to process the feelings that arise. Use the journal prompts for this week to begin to make connections between your feelings, why they're present, and what actions are needed to prioritize your needs.

# My mind was designed to think in complex ways.

**SELF-CARE GOAL:** Honor my mind's natural need to think things through at length by creating space to process my thoughts.

How does being busy or constantly multitasking influence my mental state?

_____

_____

_____

_____

_____

_____

_____

_____

_____

_____

_____

_____

When I create space to process, the quality of my thoughts is . . .

_____

_____

_____

_____

_____

_____

_____

_____

_____

_____

_____

_____

_____

_____

_____

_____

_____

_____

_____

_____

_____

_____

_____

_____

_____

Highly sensitive people are often accused of "overthinking," when really their brains are simply wired to process more. Intentionally create space to think through this week by spending a few minutes each day writing down or recording how you feel. Reflect on anything and everything that comes into your mind, without worry about grammar or content, and then answer this week's journal prompts once more, using a separate piece of paper if you have filled up this week's entry space..

## I can feel my stress and anxiety melting away.

**SELF-CARE GOAL:** Find a comfort object to help myself feel safe and relaxed during times of stress, anxiety, or feeling overwhelmed.

When I engage with this object, I notice my stress levels . . .

_____

_____

_____

_____

_____

_____

_____

_____

_____

_____

This comfort object is soothing because . . .

_____

_____

_____

_____

_____

_____

_____

_____

_____

_____

_____

_____

_____

_____

_____

And it reminds me of . . .

_____

_____

_____

_____

_____

_____

_____

_____

_____

_____

Over the next week, try out a few different comfort objects—
such as weighted blankets, stuffed animals, or fidget toys—
whenever you notice your stress levels or emotions increasing.
Notice how each object alters your mood and think back
to the week's journal prompts to determine which types of
objects are best for you and when.

# I am free to step away and prioritize my needs whenever I need to.

**SELF-CARE GOAL:** Manage energy and stimulation during a social event by taking regular breaks away from the crowd/noise.

When I step away from the group, I notice . . .

_____

_____

_____

_____

_____

_____

_____

_____

_____

_____

_____

What differences do I sense in my mood and energy after I take stimulation breaks?

_____

_____

_____

_____

_____

_____

_____

_____

_____

_____

Seek quiet refuge during a social event wherever it is available—
a restroom, outdoors, a space where you can spend time with a
pet, a spare bedroom, your car, or an empty conference room.
Take a few minutes to breathe and come back to yourself
before returning to the gathering. Repeat this process hourly
or as often as needed throughout the event.

# I am blessed by and connected to the greater world around me.

**SELF-CARE GOAL:** Rekindle or deepen a connection with a religious, spiritual, or personal practice that is meaningful to me.

What types of practices help me feel inspired and connected to the world around me?

_____

_____

_____

_____

_____

_____

_____

_____

_____

_____

_____

_____

Connecting with this practice is important to me because . . .

_____

_____

_____

_____

_____

_____

_____

_____

_____

_____

_____

_____

_____

---

---

---

---

---

---

---

---

---

Engage your spiritual side this week by connecting with your community, attending a relevant service, engaging in ritual, reading inspiring texts, or connecting with a spiritual mentor. Other options could include spending time in nature, going to the theater, visiting an art museum, connecting with animals, or any other experience that invokes feelings of inspiration and deep connection with the world around you.

# *All of my feelings are real and valid.*

**SELF-CARE GOAL:** Practice validating all my emotions and begin to transform any negative internal dialogue about "feeling too much."

What messages have I received about my "big" feelings?

_____

_____

_____

_____

_____

_____

_____

_____

_____

_____

_____

_____

How does it feel to offer myself validation?

_____

_____

_____

_____

_____

_____

_____

_____

_____

_____

_____

_____

_____

_____

_____

_____

_____

_____

_____

_____

_____

_____

_____

_____

_____

_____

Anytime you feel a strong emotion arise, notice what thoughts and sensations are present. If there are negative messages about feeling "too much" or being "too sensitive," offer yourself validation instead by repeating the week's affirmation. This mindset shift will take time to integrate, so you will find it helpful to revisit this validation practice often.

## *I will take all the time I need to make this important decision.*

**SELF-CARE GOAL:** Honor my need as a highly sensitive person to mentally process by carving out time to think over an important decision.

What typically happens when I rush to make a decision?

_____

_____

_____

_____

_____

_____

_____

_____

_____

_____

_____

_____

How does slowing down to make a decision affect the outcome?

_____

_____

_____

_____

_____

_____

_____

_____

_____

_____

_____

_____

_____

_____

_____

_____

_____

_____

_____

_____

_____

_____

_____

_____

_____

_____

Next time you have an important decision to make, reserve time to really think the situation through. You could write a pros and cons list, observe what feelings come up when you imagine each choice, or reflect on similar past experiences. Notice any pressure from within yourself or from others to move quickly, then remind yourself what's helpful about honoring your own decision-making time line.

*Taking this short break now will help me feel more productive and relaxed later.*

**SELF-CARE GOAL:** Begin to track signs of overstimulation (irritability, fatigue, headache, etc.) and take breaks regularly or as needed.

I know I need a break when . . .

_____

_____

_____

_____

_____

_____

_____

_____

_____

_____

What differences do I notice on days when I take breaks versus days when I don't prioritize my needs?

_____

_____

_____

_____

_____

_____

_____

_____

_____

_____

_____

_____

_____

_____

_____

_____

_____

_____

_____

_____

_____

_____

_____

_____

Set a recurring timer on your phone or build time into your schedule to check in with how you're feeling. If you notice any of the signs of overstimulation mentioned in this week's goal, take a break. A break can be as simple as briefly closing your eyes, or taking a few moments to sit quietly, stretch, breathe, or whatever you're needing.

*My needs are valuable, and I take responsibility for communicating them to others.*

**SELF-CARE GOAL:** Practice communicating my unique needs directly to others instead of giving subtle hints or hoping they will notice without me saying anything.

When someone does not anticipate my needs, I feel . . .

_____

_____

_____

_____

_____

_____

_____

_____

_____

When I share my needs directly, I feel . . .

_____

_____

_____

_____

_____

_____

_____

_____

_____

_____

_____

_____

_____

_____

_____

_____

_____

_____

_____

_____

_____

_____

_____

_____

_____

Those who are not highly sensitive are not as perceptive of nonverbal cues or as quick to anticipate the needs of others as HSPs are. Therefore, it's important to express your needs directly. Start by making simple requests of someone you trust, such as asking to eat at a quiet table at a restaurant or requesting a moment to think during a conversation.

*I am aware of the present moment and my experience in it.*

**SELF-CARE GOAL:** Begin a simple meditation practice to increase mindfulness of my internal experience and my connection to the universe or the world around me.

When I sit quietly with myself, I notice . . .

_____

_____

_____

_____

_____

_____

_____

_____

_____

_____

What is different about me as a result of my meditation practice?

_____

_____

_____

_____

_____

_____

_____

_____

_____

_____

_____

_____

_____

_____

_____

_____

_____

_____

_____

_____

_____

_____

_____

_____

For two to five minutes each day—or longer if you're a seasoned meditator—sit quietly in a comfortable seated or reclined position. Focus your attention on your breath moving in and out as you slowly repeat this week's affirmation. Without judgment, note any thoughts, emotions, or sensations that arise. You may find it helpful to refer to the mindfulness tools in the resources list on page 158.

# I am in control of soothing my emotions.

**SELF-CARE GOAL:** Stay present with my emotions as they happen and learn to recognize what tools I have for self-soothing these feelings.

In the past, what has helped me manage my emotions and feel calm again?

_____

_____

_____

_____

_____

_____

_____

_____

_____

_____

_____

_____

Are there different tools that feel effective for different feelings?

_____

_____

_____

_____

_____

_____

_____

_____

_____

_____

_____

_____

_____

_____

_____

_____

_____

_____

_____

_____

_____

_____

_____

Reflecting on past experiences, what typically feels comforting when you're agitated, angry, or overwhelmed? What about when you are sad or grieving? Start to make a list of what tools are in your emotional regulation toolbox and when they are effective. Some examples are going for a walk or otherwise moving your body in any way that feels good to you, journaling about your experience, naming what you see around you, breathing mindfully, and running your hands under cool water.

# My mind feels satisfied when I learn something new.

**SELF-CARE GOAL:** Study a topic I am interested in or want to increase my awareness of, such as a historical event, influential person, or new language.

What did I learn this week about my topic of interest?

_____

_____

_____

_____

_____

_____

_____

_____

_____

_____

_____

Did I learn anything new about myself?

_____

_____

_____

_____

_____

_____

_____

_____

_____

_____

_____

_____

_____

_____

_____

_____

_____

_____

_____

_____

_____

_____

_____

_____

_____

_____

Highly sensitive people often feel bored when they aren't getting enough intellectual stimulation. This week, choose a subject you would feel excited to study and then collect your materials. You may want to check out books from the library, find an online course, or attend a local class. Whatever avenue you choose, how you feel during the process is more important than what you're learning.

## I feel engaged and entertained without looking at a screen.

**SELF-CARE GOAL:** Reduce overstimulation from screen time and replace it with quiet downtime or more tactile activities.

When I spend all day looking at a screen, I feel . . .

_____

_____

_____

_____

_____

_____

_____

_____

_____

_____

_____

_____

During screen breaks, I notice . . .

_____

_____

_____

_____

_____

_____

_____

_____

_____

_____

_____

_____

_____

_____

_____

_____

_____

_____

_____

_____

_____

_____

_____

_____

Spend some time each day without any screen time. You can start small with just a few minutes and build up to as much time as you need. Be sure to have a few alternative activities lined up, such as puzzle books, reading materials, or art supplies.

*While I am more attuned to the needs of others, I must also ask for what I need.*

**SELF-CARE GOAL:** Acknowledge and manage feelings of resentment when someone misses my subtle cues for support or attention, and then express my needs directly.

What is difficult about not having my needs anticipated?

_____

_____

_____

_____

_____

_____

_____

_____

_____

How do I feel when I express my needs and that request is granted?

_____

_____

_____

_____

_____

_____

_____

_____

_____

_____

_____

_____

_____

_____

_____

_____

_____

_____

_____

_____

_____

_____

_____

_____

It's easy for highly sensitive people to feel resentful for giving too much in relationships and not having that gesture reciprocated. It's important to validate those feelings and then see if it feels right to express your needs directly. This week, practice clearly stating your needs with people you trust. Reflect on how it felt to make those needs known and the results you saw from expressing yourself.

*My energy is clear; I know what energy is mine and what energy is not mine.*

**SELF-CARE GOAL:** Become more conscious of the energy I pick up from others and create a boundary to protect myself.

What tells me that an emotion or sensation is not mine?

_____

_____

_____

_____

_____

_____

_____

_____

_____

How can I best release the emotion and return to my own emotional experience?

_____

_____

_____

_____

_____

_____

_____

_____

_____

_____

_____

_____

_____

_____

_____

_____

_____

_____

_____

_____

_____

_____

_____

_____

_____

_____

Because they are so empathetic and perceptive, HSPs often feel like they are absorbing the emotions of others. Next time you are with another person, notice any signs that what you're feeling is not yours—such as when an emotion comes out of nowhere or doesn't make sense based on your recent experiences. Practice saying "not mine" to yourself and visualize gently giving the person their energy back.

# *I take great delight in the little joys of my life.*

**SELF-CARE GOAL:** Begin to notice and pause on the small moments that bring me joy throughout the day.

Today I felt happy when . . .

_____

_____

_____

_____

_____

_____

_____

_____

_____

_____

_____

This moment reminded me of . . .

_____

_____

_____

_____

_____

_____

_____

_____

_____

_____

_____

_____

_____

_____

_____

_____

_____

_____

_____

_____

_____

_____

_____

_____

_____

_____

Feeling deeply as a highly sensitive person is an advantage that allows you to be greatly affected by the little pleasures in life, such as hearing a bird singing, enjoying a delicious snack, receiving a smile from a stranger, and so on. Whenever you catch any glimpse of joy over the next week, take a moment to pause and let it soak in.

## *My sensitivity is a gift with many strengths (even when I may feel overwhelmed).*

**SELF-CARE GOAL:** Begin to rewrite the message that I am "too sensitive" and identify at least one strength in having the highly sensitive trait.

When someone says "you're too sensitive" to me, I feel . . .

_____

_____

_____

_____

_____

_____

_____

_____

_____

_____

My sensitivity is a gift because . . .

_____

_____

_____

_____

_____

_____

_____

_____

_____

_____

_____

_____

_____

_____

_____

_____

_____

_____

_____

_____

_____

_____

_____

_____

_____

Over the next week, notice when being highly sensitive is actually an advantage. For example, being naturally more empathetic helps you support friends in need, and being more perceptive allows you to catch critical mistakes at work. Noticing details, being wired to pause and reflect instead of quickly making decisions, and having greater intuition also come in handy. When in doubt, repeat this week's affirmation to yourself.

# RESOURCES

## HIGHLY SENSITIVE PERSON SELF-TEST

Use this self-test to understand the different components of the trait and what you personally experience as an HSP. It's also helpful to pass this along to friends, family members, and coworkers as a point of discussion and connection. You can take the adult and child HSP test at HSPerson.com/test

## *THE HIGHLY SENSITIVE PERSON* BY DR. ELAINE ARON

A must-read for every HSP, this is the book that introduced high sensitivity to the world. This book will provide you with deep insights into what it means to be highly sensitive and how the trait affects you personally, and it also contains helpful tips that will help you navigate many areas of your life with more ease.

## *SENSITIVE: THE UNTOLD STORY* DOCUMENTARY

Watching this documentary is both a visually engaging way to learn about the trait and an easy way to introduce your sensitivity to a friend or loved one. You can watch it online at SensitiveTheMovie.com.

## *MINDFULNESS WORKBOOK FOR STRESS RELIEF* BY APRIL SNOW, LMFT

Learn the powerful benefits of mindfulness, as well as practical and accessible tools to begin or reconnect with your practice.

## INSIGHT TIMER

Sometimes you need a little guidance to help you practice self-care. The Insight Timer app is my favorite resource for guided meditation and mindfulness exercises. Download the app at InsightTimer.com.

## THE BETTER BOUNDARIES WORKBOOK
## BY SHARON MARTIN, LCSW

The ability to set boundaries is an essential skill for every HSP to ensure they get enough downtime. This book will help you explore the difficult emotions around and practical tips for setting limits.

## THE MINDFUL SELF-COMPASSION WORKBOOK
## BY KRISTIN NEFF, PHD, AND CHRISTOPHER GERMER, PHD

Deepening your capacity for self-compassion will help you transform the negative messages you've internalized about being highly sensitive and begin treating yourself with kindness and acceptance instead.

## BEFRIENDING YOUR NERVOUS SYSTEM
## BY DEB DANA, LCSW

As a highly sensitive person, the biggest obstacle to thriving is often feeling physically overstimulated. This book will guide you through how to tend to your sensitive nervous system and soothe overwhelming emotions.

## MEETUP GROUPS

Connecting with other highly sensitive people is important to feeling deeply understood and coming to accept your trait, but it can often be difficult to know where to find community. Thankfully there are many options locally and online. Start by searching Meetup.com for HSP gatherings in your area.

## MORE RESOURCES

You can find additional HSP-specific resources on my website at SensitiveStrengths.com.

# REFERENCES

Acevedo, Bianca P., Elaine N. Aron, Arthur Aron, Matthew-Donald Sangster, Nancy Collins, and Lucy L. Brown. "The Highly Sensitive Brain: An fMRI Study of Sensory Processing Sensitivity and Response to Others' Emotions." *Brain and Behavior* 4, no. 4 (June 2014): 580–94. doi.org/10.1002/brb3.242.

Belsky, Jay, and Michael Pluess. "Beyond Diathesis Stress: Differential Susceptibility to Environmental Influences." *Psychological Bulletin* 135, no. 6 (2009): 885–908. doi.org/10.1037/a0017376.

Lionetti, Francesca, Arthur Aron, Elaine N. Aron, G. Leonard Burns, Jadzia Jagiellowicz, and Michael Pluess. "Dandelions, Tulips, and Orchids: Evidence for the Existence of Low-Sensitive, Medium-Sensitive, and High-Sensitive Individuals." *Translational Psychiatry* 8, no. 24 (2018). doi.org/10.1038/s41398-017-0090-6.

# ABOUT THE AUTHOR

 **APRIL SNOW, LMFT,** is a licensed psycho-
therapist, author, and consultant in California
who specializes in working with highly sensitive
introverts to help them overcome the stress and
anxiety of living in a busy, overwhelming world.

Using mindfulness, self-compassion, journaling, and other experiential practices, she helps
clients fully understand their unique needs, release feelings of guilt that
arise from prioritizing those needs, and start creating a life on their own
terms so that their sensitive strengths can shine through.

Deeply committed to changing the narrative of what it means to be
highly sensitive and understanding firsthand the powerful impact of community, April has created and led HSP workshops and retreats all over the
country, as well as online through her Sensitive School.

To learn more and access a variety of resources for highly sensitive
introverts and highly sensitive therapists, visit SensitiveStrengths.com.